THE RED BIRD

Joyelle McSweeney

FENCEbooks

Cover photograph by   Keith Meyers / NYT Pictures

Author Photo by   Shannon Welch

Published in the United States by

       Fence Books   Saturnalia Books
       14 Fifth Avenue, #1A   87 E. 2nd St., #5A
       New York, NY 10011   New York, NY 10003
       www.fencebooks.com   www.saturnaliabooks.com

Book design by   Saturnalia Books

Fence Books is distributed by   University Press of New England
                                           www.upne.com

Library of Congress Cataloguing in Publication Data
    McSweeney, Joyelle [1976–]
    The Red Bird / Joyelle McSweeney

Library of Congress Control Number: 2002103593

ISBN 0-9713189-0-5

FIRST EDITION

The author gratefully acknowledges the journals *Jubilat*, *The Boston Review*, *Perihelion* and *Fence* for publishing her work, as well as the patience of her parents and the kindness of her friends and teachers.

Printed in Canada.

For Brette, Ross, and Keeffe

TABLE OF CONTENTS

Foreword

A poet must give her readers (for their trouble) something worth having. The best gift a poet can give is truth to the fact of experience—hard to get at and rare to find. In the poems of Joyelle McSweeney you will discover the art of a resolute mind, intent on making plain in words what there is to see, to know, to feel in her world, in her time—which is yours and mine. Her title—*The Red Bird*—names that resolute mind.

Joyelle McSweeney's poetry is concerned neither with extreme experience, nor with commonplace. She is a poetic realist. Her poems are neither reductive nor fantastic. But they are profoundly mysterious in the way any truthful account of the world must be. Joyelle McSweeney is a poet with a vocation—a calling to the world. What is given her (the vocation) is to make others see what is given her to see:

> *What do ye do when ye see a whale?*
> I sing out.

This is the moment (in her word) of "veridical" seeing. But it is, also, as important to her (as much a part of her truth) to say (precisely) what she cannot see. For example,

> . . . I embrace you, and I admit
> that internal suffering is difficult to photograph.

The Red Bird contributes, not experience, but awareness of experience. McSweeney knows exactly how to say what her poetry adds to the world of her readers:

> It adds to the perfection of what was already known
> the spectrality of the heated object.
> It is rapidly becoming
> the brightest thing in the sky.

The value of the poetry of *The Red Bird* (awareness, without dismay, of the facts of the world) is the same value we attribute to our own thought, when we think well. The contribution of McSweeney's poetry is that it supplies the warrant for doing so. Such is the inestimable value of the engaged realist in poetry, or any art.

—Allen Grossman

Still Life w/ Influences

I stood at the modern knothole,
my eyes on the pivoting modern stars and naphthalene green
turfs and surfaces.

Behind me the stone fleur-de-lis
sank back over the horizon,
carving a fleur-de-lis-shaped track in air
that spread into a bigger hole.

                       Up on the hill,
a white tent had just got unsteadily to its feet
like a foal or a just-foaled cathedral.
Down on the beach, ten black whales were crashing

slowly, through themselves,
draped in wet bedsheets.
The bedsheets smoked into the air.

I opened my palm. A green edifice opened there.
It seemed to breathe but that was air breathing for it,
lifting a corner or a column.

Goodbye, my thirteenth-century.
                   I folded the money away.
What do ye do when ye see a whale?
                 I sing out.

Toy House

It lay on the sheet, I waited for it to move
under the grainy roof.

Plus, I measured the house it measured a reed
I measured the gate, a reed.

The angel intervened just once in all this time,
carrying my voice twelve miles. My rider came back
and took more formal leave.

I was plucky as the mail coach I was also the mud
that caught the letters dropping. That was the angel talking.

I say Wolves removed
to the lodgpole pine forests, can you
see those mudcaked hooves

Developed Nation

Is this how a god returns from victory?

This is *america*. The boy soprano
into the doughnut-world.
Fresh from the fish-mold.
Clattering out across the snow
          to buy a paperknife,
clutching a flier. . .

A test in *harmonies*.
Here comes the perfect pitch—
it's white, it falls to the glove,
showing its stitches. Here comes
the hot-front, stitched with flags

O beautiful he produceth
language from everyplace
on his body, the room
where the heatcloud lifts to the ceiling. . .

the subcommander crouched in the stalkbed breathing
into his lily-season

My Brother-in-Law, Frank Hunger

We huddled over the audiocast.
Frank rose to adjust the volume
as if making a dream concession. . .

Peace in the horn. . .
Peace in the horn of Africa!
Our new technician

brings in two-hundred-fifty thousand dollars a year
in color work. she says they want lots of glimmer.
they want *lashes*.
Whereupon the editor says *adieu*.

Ginned clean of seeds, packed into bales
through a season of ten-dollar hours. . .
who is it sleeps in these sheets?

Sleeps in the bale, sleeps in the parcel
of coveted land, over one thousand acres
in the park's interior. Sleeps
its construction, its disrepair, a discussion
in two out of three magnet schools,
in which the magnet is *history*. . .

It adds to the perfection of what was already known
the spectrality of the heated object.
It is rapidly becoming
the brightest thing in the sky.

The New Island

1. Four persistent concerns remain:
the primary claim, appearances, the emptiness,
credibility;

drive x erased and the mapping deleted.
drive y deleted and the mapping erased.

how to give expression to this feeling. could one part
of earth be holier than all. could one part
with earth for these viridical visions. Broccoli
in the desert. Billboard moon. On the strength of these

eighteenwheelers! "Being Founder of the Church
took something visually perceptible. . ." how a bath here
makes one feel: beyond words

2. *Pro se* for him *pro nobis* for us; such is
the language of heav'nly indication.

Divine intentions as such immediately
cause effects. Kept secret, *in pectore*, little lava gull,
it happens just the same. little crime rate. little shoe.

and one wonders whether the crime rate here in Brabant
can justify such a *Palais de Justice*
as this one, won in competition. to represent

oneself in civil cases: *pro se*

3. Did you forget my friend Pluto?
From world's smallest planet to King of the Kuiper Belt!
tant mieux, he is always saying. *quelque chose là haut.*
what could equal a life in the Hook of Holland.
a drawing that will be understood by everyone.
as my creditors know, zero *articles de luxe*

in this house. But here's Mirabile (Face Turned). Her right hand
luminous and songful; at other times lightly veiled.
Her other name is Naturelle.

In this drawing, the light flows from heaven
just exactly as it does in the world itself.

4. Inanycase: an increase in the value of objects
with time can be depended on. My brother
foisting the chest-on-chest
off on some other American. It refuses to fit
through the door. All day they've been tennissing.

They've been negotiating for a little theophany
under the table, don't you know. The only thing we want
is to have what we've done matter. going from one place
with a problem to the next place with a problem. . . .

the spaces are connected so that
ascent and descent are not only
unnoticable but at the same time

functional. And every agent wants
to make something like himself.
Omni agens agit sibi simile. . .

to represent himself

5. What's life
without the prophetic/hope trajectory.
without the throne/vision trajectory.
With the success of the anti-corruption platform,
the Graves Project. The bodies open into the field
and the field into the river.

It's been discovered
that rice can serve as model for the life of crops
which defy easy sequencing.

A stunning vitamin victory. . .
Underswell of a marine inquiry. . .

the farmbuildings the sheds the watertanks the little horses
all seem to be called up

The Idealized Landscape

*

Noon robbery; the stalkflower gets bluer
in the beds outside the bank. It's been
a superb day. The longest growing season
on the Atlantic coast. A handwritten note
slid under the portcullis, the teller reading it
for a long time

*

A new moon is an unrealized moon! Last night,
the wrestlers stood like two moons
on either side of the ref. Today, a new field blooms
through the test-well; a flapping flame
above the floating platform, a just-detected gift
recalling its passage, reciting it

*

. . . .a maze of beams and cables, the end
of the electrified railroad line, slopes
of the Blue Mountains.

A condor with twice my wingspan glided by
overhead. He made the planes. I named the teas

and wrote canister copy. *'Some meaningfulness
in clothes. . .' 'or in the hidden gate. . .' 'something just
coagulating out of air. . .'*

*

This fish likes to live in deep salt water.
Gasses sluff about on the surface of the sun,
superheating the corona. The sun shines.

Violence erupts at the sacred center.
My father emerges from his coma
speaking his pet language.

The auditorium opened, he makes arrangements
to buy back the year's entire crop.

*

No one can smoke inside this car, inside this vitrine
composition. Outside, the web of tenthousand things;
inside here, only three: filmstrip of a helicopter's shadow;
against an Antarctic wall; silkscreen
of the grand central ceiling. The idealized landscape—
I want a room in it.

Toy Bed

The bobcat poses in a tripod of rifles.
The crown of the emperor penguin slips down halfway
over his eyes. Light shades down bluely from the ice cliff

to the ice. Now this
is a salt marsh, but this can't have salt
or glass. The black wool beret is sodden and itches
and pushes my wet bangs down into my eyes
in little points. The field is flooded, floodened.
This has lost

its ice and good light. I slipped into the channel,
my thin nylon jacket soaked through right away with mud.
Mud pouched in snaky curls inside it. I stood up.
Is there still time to walk

out, pitch a stick and read the current, fold back
the green felt cap, poke a feather through, remove
myself to higher ground? Inside the dry house, thinking
What does the deer do, now, in the woods? He wears

a too-huge stylized rack. It pulls his head back
black-lipped to the sky, or pulls his head down
and he must graze and brood. It pulls
his lips and makes him smile. It closes his eyes.

Toy Enterprise

The fake barn is made of a light-loving resin.
On the dark hill, it seems to float. In fact floats.
We drag in what we think might sell.

The guitarist with the burnt forearm,
the drummer fished up out of the world in which he was immersed,
the other guitarist who had fallen into furniture design

conversant. We then commence
a seven-hour gunfight, slow, schematic.
We rewrite the code to draw it out,
to keep it happening. Meanwhile,
baseball and everything goes on in one city.
Closing prices blossom from the shut city's fist.
How the day ended.

what's over
is packed inside the replicated ship:
    a stone oil lamp, a soapstone spindle, shiprivets, a bone needle,
    the Vikings' generally healthy lives.
The ship itself is suspended. When

the vocalist arrives and unlocks the door
we clock out.
He drives me down to the sharp end of the isthmus.
Sheets of green water bolt up over the sand
and fall back. Then up in a plane. we make plans
to ride horseback down the rice-levees. It's dove season.

Toy Election

It's important. The gleaners demand it
picking over the field for tiny grains.
The children are at home, being polled.
A roof-top grape has been coaxed to fizz
delicately, there will be a tiny appellation.

Should we, and should we
in long or short walks or running
or should we cinched with backup ropes
of hemp, nylon and sisal
about which we are religious?

My fellow dolphins implore me
to take part in a game
called "fish-fetch opportunities."
I can watch my character
succeed to the different boards.
This going in

and indoors, this being
clad and clad.
I know no word
better than orchard.

Toy Maternity

Last year, like so many others
he bought racehorses on the bull market.
The darlings deflated

en masse. So I debuted
on next to nothing, one slipper
on the Turkish carpet,

half bustle and half wig.
The rescue vessel sinks itself
by filling its ballast tanks, slips

under the listing vessel, then surfaces
cargo and all. Therefore
he who believes in me

goes into me
and he who goes into me
has me. I of course refer

to that fleet of buried ships
the fourteen yellow prows
that carried the Pharaoh to the afterlife

and came back
mostly rotted, and to the smallest
body ever

orbited
that closest
that primitive body

Developed Nation

The ornament free and self-propelling.
A-round in the plastic globe!
a gift from our number-one employer,

The Sun. See you next year, faithful.
The billboard cowboy working
and the landscape working as well. Progression

at the same rate. How to/
how not to tell. they walked
our plane out over the highway.
wind underneath, bright wind
shields,
       the body
slips through the heated field
and, spinning,
generates. My face

in the oval window. the invisible
hole in the invisible
not opening.

Roman

what are robberies but little kingdoms?
on that and other intramurals, no idea.
on the prayers of the commerce secretary,
on the freight train hit the freight train
que ferai-je sans Eurydice no idea.

+

let me tell you about fortune. It means
things which have no cause, such that
causes do not proceed them. c.f.
Japan as No. 1; c.f. secrets enough
to bring this republic down twenty times over.
          ".Rave Capital of Europe"—the two guys
saying it at once, or else the space between them
opening up and saying
          I just saw bam bam
          like a bright muzzle flame
          from both guns at once
          obliterated my vision

+

The assembly is *not* out of reach.
The dog falls like an angel,
burlap-cauled.

Let him keep his opinion. But correct
his language. For why does he not
say at first what he will say afterwards—
when someone shall put to him the question—

avant-rive ou rive gauche ou rive
everywhereandwherever
that perfect music lives

+

So all ears which are coeval or
so to speak cogerminal some
destroyed by mildew some
devoured by birds and some pulled up; so

goes my coloratura, my cantata
for the twenty-seventh Sunday after Lent and so
goes my cantabile.

My Cantabile:

+

(The bloodfeud was once the primary mechanism)
(of social order)
(the worldover.)

(Each arrow they sent over my stockade fence)
(guess who)
(it pointed to)

+

Shown and rejected/the giver of trees'/
glory/ the eternal/city! Slew the eternal/
comishner of parks,/ giver of the bird manual!/

for conquest ornithological.
and he took that new man for his brother,
though he had a little brother of his own.

had lights earth fruit an *empire* of his own.

+

Calvary Officers!
This is just the next step.

I admit; I did not show my usual sagacity
in choosing this course; this violent mem'ry route;
when you lift the skin, each joint of the hand
corresponds to one of twenty-three places.

not the usual sagacity. on my father's roof,
the scope we used to see objects beyond the galaxy.
that full scope might be given to his expansive compassion:

opened the doors. that a large multitude might
shelter there—*find* shelter there—"I come not
with love but with a granary. . ."

Abusive odyssey.

+

"it seemed obvious to us that we should make use
of natural shapes: leaves, branches twigs. . ."

And if I were founding a new city,
I could build on the order of nature.
But since I am only finding one,
I must

"But as you walk around a quarter-turn,
the *flowers* appear to change.
A second layer of ornament.
Something totally else revealed."

+

I was a mockingbird a makebate a malcontented guest I made my way
against the continent, starting with the first gorge, starting out with a
picture of a swimming shrimp transparent in a sea of black I tucked it
everywhere. It was National; Geographic; I thought myself lapseless in
that pre-Louisian state but there *was* a map; it kept extending itself from
the cover, the same beautiful accident repeated to no loss of effect and
from that point onward *I could not pretend*

+

Defamation, and falsehood, but no malice.
Such were the findings of the court.

I guess the public's not ready for what we could show to it.

Got seriously ill during halftime.
Got counterfeit shares and worth nothing.

It took the Discordia Concourse.
It took the trompettes-de-la-mort
and the world as a vast divine system of metaphors

to keep me operating.
to keep me a going concern.

Elba

I could not get used
to the disaster. Watching Burden of Proof
with my surrogate-elect.

The English pirate better known as.
In a battle off Virginia.
Preceded in death. Death claimed her

at her house. We were
dropped off at the FBI outpost since
our schoolbus could get no further.

The agents fanning out across the snow. . .

Here in the departure lounge
with the rest of the unconfirmed passengers
        talking guitars,
renewals, tarte renversee, the corporate
string tones, a tiny curving stage
what the big stars would say

of our million-dollar views.
of the mille lacs.
A pattern in language, a grammar of ornament, decoration
expressing concealment, response to facts, such as

Replay the sequence: the car flips and then
the car flips.
Because of this
budget the project was mostly composition
and arrangement. Open the cake bible. Stop her
shrinking into her coat.

I realized there was no more flying in this airplane.
My story goes: dropping chocolate bars
into tiny hands. Which would go on to perfect
the cloth-covered table the interrogator's lamp

Elba

The maid shows up to find it in its beds.
Young, suffocated,
shy of its birthdays.

Fallen trees. The stadiums are designed
to be flooded. Beaten glass is designed
to be nontransparent.

Virgin-Mother: I must have
happened without happening to keep you that way.
Keep me good or at least lucky. Dear Madam I'm

able. I was.
Ere I saw
God in the detail

of your fine brocade, Lady-at-the-Virginal.
It shines and makes everything shine.
A view of Delft. The dull side of the foil.
What we were before

in the nursery, crying and crying out artlessly
in front of one another,
in our beds or on the toilet

What are you inside of now,
a nut? This film of heat
unwrapping from the styrofoam cup?

A heron rows itself across the sky.
I need to tell you this while you're asleep.
The noise was a real noise
          but not in a real place.

Persuasion

Others were more economical than I. But I
had my red marble. I had action
figures weighting down the drapes
on tiny threads. That twisted and got smaller.
One door led
to a more economical room.
Perhaps a more economical view. The girl
across the hall was the same girl.

I climbed out across the telephone wires. I thought
they'd hold me, like the webbing of a lawn chair,
and like a wedding or a lawnchair they didn't. I kept
pulling chunks out of the hummock. I fell with my
fists full of humus. Into, of course.

At home the state-painter was painting the ghost oak. And
the window around the oak. The room around

you-know-who.
She came from the same
town in Iceland.
Whither and whence I
came. O-ho!
With her eye
she came and came.
With her weather
eye she came.

I saw the damage this was doing to the van
would *not* cost six hundred dollars.
I pedaled off in my car.
My car got smaller.
It wouldn't fit my littlest brother!
It fell over.
Fell, of course, into.

Back at the ranch, it was a tenement.
I was a tenant of the studio-apartment.
I was building a house in French.
Expectorant—I was self-enlightened,
my efforts self-directed and sustained.
To the tune of eighty-seven dollars
I debated a suitable depth. A squirrel
at each level of the fence

with an apple for a face looked on blandly.
I mean red. Red-faced. Blindly.

Heavenly stage set comes
in on wheels and wheels around.
The fish wind up the concrete ladder
because they believe it's better
to reach a higher part of the *rive*.
to pour themselves out
while I pour myself into

the form that has survived.
my father leaves tomorrow
and he leaves this
afternoon. This is before
I set fire to my room,
pouring water into the electric baseboards
trying to wash a tiny brine shrimp
off the wall. It might have lived.
This is after my mother,
her father dead. Lay in bed.
Heard the Skylark song.

Animal Instruction

ha! a perfect bear! —from 'Dead Souls'

1.
The saint of bears
should be your saint.
Your nameday lined in red.
Where is your trumpet and your tiny hat?
You go by Misha
in the Russian imagination
on honey and black bread.
You live in the march
in splendid hibernation
You live on the sedgy strip.

2.
At the postmaster's soiree
I wanted to be filled
as with risotto
I wanted to be over
dancing the postillion
just leaning back
The wrist came uncovered
when the hand grasped mine
On the hole at the neck
of the regimental cufflink
I rested my eye
The breeze lifts the wing
of a hawk struck dead
along the center line

3.
Space Ghost, recitative!
Now, Space Ghost, *pas de deux!*
The audience starts
and starts applauding. In this scene

I am the general. I can issue
my own voice. Attn., miniplanets!
This threadbare dachshund fears for
the automaker's collapse!
This piny dacha welcomes
the messenger in the mushroom cap!

He squeezes up through the floorboards.
He says Don't you recognize me?
He glares at the drop-leaf table. He says,
Didn't you get my gift?

4.
The stork flaps around the kitchen.
The color of the plaster ceiling,
it grinds one wing around
It makes the motion meaning
'Roll your window down!'
The yellow eye boiling, the
beak pointing blackly to the floor
it goes over it again, and again
nothing is skipped

Premiers

1.
We get in, the drummer has cancer.
his palms break open halfway through the set.
He's up in the cage, bleeding, we jump up and down
in the crowd breaking up. *Lunation. Synodic month.*
I look up. Pendant of red wolves
hung behind the chapel. Pendant, inset, with Alps.

2.
The ship enters harbor and switches to civil time.
Vermin of various sizes traverse the mooring ropes.
Point q to point Q. Dr. Query,
we were never aligned with the Polestar,
the moon caused repetitive wobblings, for centuries
we were wrong. The sun stands still briefly, heads south.
One looks off through a long swath of atmosphere
at sunrise—alternatively, at moonrise—which distorts.

3.
Now we must return to find our hometown
under gold, the town a vault, a post-season
record for wild-pitches, a crackdown on cricket-sparring,
the cold-lipped general gloved, awaiting word.
Chestnuts make sugar from their starches, a dog retrieves.
Little stones knock around in the hollow for a reason
such as the hollow is magnetic. Snow kestrels come back.

The Premier

On a wave of resignations and dismissals without precedent
I rode in. I drove in from Connecticut. I was called in.
I sanded down graffiti from the door
of my concert box. I took the sixth seventh and eighth floors.
I stood out under the red tree and opened the preferable flesh.
I took the eighth ninth and tenth. I was deeply
in love with the building. Stings the cuts on my fingers,
rinds against my toes. A fat brown leaf
into the red minnowy leaflets drops and stops dropping.
They look down at me. A tenterhook adapted
from the linen trade, a cartilaginous collar: I rode in.
If you can't chase down your butcher for a cut of white king,
see me. If you're from hell, you're from hell, see
Fat leaf at rest in the still red tree see me. Who am
I if I mean what I sometimes mean.

The Gray Pony

It is the real October ninth. Kneebreeched,
waistcoated, I pause outside the arbor
with my black dog, Sancho. Curls and curls
of Sancho, both of our etched-on out-of-door breaths.
To which I add the smoke of my pipe

and a small boy over the stone wall
and through the arms of a hawthorn tree. Childish skirts
among the red-brown thorns, I catch him.
He is clean.
                Out comes the real lady!
She says it, I repeat it.

Later, at tea,
a lady's actions will go unnoticed by me
until my sister points them out.
I point this out. She is sewing the button on.
The fire rearranges itself in the grate
with a pointed sigh. Topcoat.
                Come on, Sancho!

Dusk, the rough road between manors.
I hear pines, the lady-in-the-river,
then the tramp of horse-hooves. Falls to me.
Over the wall, over the field, down to the lane
I meet him. *You're hurting my pony's mouth!*
It is not so. But I let the bridle go. What holds me
rooted, then lifts me

collar-wise over the fence?
The ground is chapped. I slip back to my own
bed and my cornfields, my elevated regions.
Out on the hill with the reapers.
A light wind over the corn.
'Just step across to this neighboring field,'
I hear the gray pony thinking—
pale cheek, eye glittering—

By morning, Sancho is back.

Assembling the Birds

In thick coverts
I carried it in my mouth, at times biting it
to change my mouth around. A hole had been prepared.
I circled the hole and dropped it in.
I filled the hole back in. What I now know
that I did not know, addresses me. The river,
for one. The four torn-up birds

I had just left Storm King School
with my bad ankle taped
        and my new white clothes
the roaring in the channel
        the dusty white wake
and a picture of my boat
        I looked for my boat

The exercise
She performed the exercise,
submitted to a higher authority, received,
executed orders, and in this evolution
got bigger. Not the hand of God
but the hand of Diego tipped
this ball into its goal. Now a dory rocks up
to a ship in the harbor. The ship gets bigger.
The dory disappears. The next day,
the hole in the hull appears
to have somehow grown bigger.

Assembling the birds
Dove carved from the granary ridgepole
and flagstaff eagle, wings stiff blades.
The eagle, for safety. Arrows in his talons.
The eagle with a crayon in his hand.

A garnet lantern
knocks against the Ark. The lost seascape
sinks through the seacoast underworld.
Little gems spill out from the pomegranate rind,
aquamarine and bloodstone, bloodstone and bloodjasper,
spilled up on shore. Tourmaline's to frustrate
bad decisions. Sapphire's for you, failing-eyes.

The Round Table

The bass had pilfered a Shadrap not long before,
& Dave & I laughed in amazement

in Quart Grave's kidney:
four adrenaline-secreting cancers.
filing the countervailing
-duty complaint one working day
after the agreement

Thanks to my partner Bill (the rain god)'s customary effect on the weather—

Could I move like a *king* crab? Six feet
wide, my six legs tearing up the ocean?
For there is the field tilled by six plows, twelve oxen.
Here is a hauberk. To make work

Two
Quart Grave: are *you* conflicted
in the Forest of Advantage, the Waste Forest?

As Perceval points out, it's impossible
for anyone to be born like this:
mailshirt, six-legged
(four equine, two your own).
Are you these angels men complain of,
who kill whatever they come upon?

We pivoted amid the swells in frantic tack
and literally surfed into the bay

Temperate, temperate-delicious,
you left your voice all over this forest.
Enabled frame-relay, this bird

like. and its beak like.

four hundred

Three
dollars for a maritime chart of the Yensai Delta.
and what was inside the envelope
we suspect keeps not existing.

I dropped a large beetlespin deep along the breakline.
Set the hook in something heavy.

Anger over the handover.
An exception that should not have!
      told my daughters:
all this shooting's because the king is getting married.

public history.
push the rock into the rock-arena.
could this site itself tour

Four
A UNIVERSAL DECLARATION!
(or, a formal ode)
with two codas and a burden line.
a bird-in-line. . .

sorry, three codas.
missed something huge

when my rod exploded from its holder on a hardstrike

(the title on the spine)
we're made to feel larger
(this sweater)
I'm made to feel in contact with it.

Whatever the nature of the regime, there's no alternative
to dialogue. Modern reindeer, a herding
to the abattoir, each diamond
carrying its own certificate

does not believe in conflict
that cannot end

Five
Supplication "makes sense" in this university town.
Conceit of: fashioning a mourning wreath
inside an intact system, ancient, and rich.
      Among your lawns and hedges/
      With scissors and shears/ I've come *The added ʒoom*
      / To force a floral opening to

Six
The knight of the cart was lost in thought.
A man with no strength nor defense.

And when it rolled to the surface, we gaped at its siʒe.
The walker-lonely chain, the weedbed.

Radio Sucre. You are the final hope of France.
This is a Penguin History.
We cannot be expected to find room

for all questions that may be asked.

Rash boon. All the palfreys neighing in the brake.
She had found a way to produce her own stringy ichor.
It tossed on the sea like blonde hair.
The dress was beautiful, and still brand new.
The tunic and mantle were still brand new.
I lost my love, but not my other love.
And now I've left the city in great shape.

Seven
Avian light, a brief command.
Had man not already begun to live for himself,
it was time now.
        —And nothing with which to cover themselves.
Striking each other in the open.

Monstrous. Monstrance, shrine maiden.
It means "exposed for veneration"
and is a global problem.
He would avenge his shame or increase it.
And return, if he would, on the third day.

If this didn't seem a gesture of arrogance before,
it did now.
        gaiatsu—pressure from the outside.
We are a patient team.
I am persuaded by his discussions of valuation.
It's humiliating and dismaying

that the battle is taking this long—

Interview With a Dog

After three nights on the mountaintop, the dog began to speak.
The night sky curved around to hear

miel, honey, mille, the thousand flours, mildly

What language is he speaking? He needs dog friends—

My sheep were nervous in the passionless state.
I'd made it halfway to the goldfields
when my vehicle burnt to the ground on its own.

when the SWAT team formed a diamond and sunk into the canyon floor.
Wedged in the dripping crevice, I watched the circles spread

knowing the right one by its soaring expense.

This is a great apparatus for the United States,
here in the Superdome. What created light?
My master's spoken word.

I've been so sick and sad about this dump forever,
making lamps for the Vatican of design firms,
accounting for, abluting,

parading outside the city wall with my crew of wild turkeys,
and my Map of the Waterholes, Lava Flows,
Dune Seas, Cinder Cones,

and Organ Pipe Cactus National Monument

and my folder of languages and temperate zones

The house-dog pleads for his liberties and mercies
Padfisted, reeling in my trunks—
this torso wants out!

Light squares off. . .
I stand at the bell for the winnowing out

The hymn-dog whispering
accounting for, abluting
this mark food left on my body
this mark a dark thought left around my eyes

and the loss of my white sheepbodies
and what was tied so tightly to my wrist

The Barque of a Million Years

I remember the first metal doorframe I came through.
My name would not be finished.
Patronym, my patronymic,

where did you think we were?
After a lively class on joints,
I climbed up to the stadium over the sea
and down to its oval floor.
Steep rows of white seats swelled.

The bright disk of a coin in my open palm.
The gilt head of my sister-prince, looking away,
drawing the extra light from day down to herself.

Her solar barque came circling overhead
zeroing in to dock.

Palm trees flipped like bones above the golfcourse.
Lightning still-framed the progress of the celestial St. Bernard
and the always restless king.

That king was me. *Open and heal, my brother-bank!*
leaving him behind, I called, *for it is better and more natural!*
Daybreak at the butter farm, dominion of horses.
Fetlocks, socks. Stripes on my sleeve, a bee there.
A face of bees assuming its solar features.

What you only *seemed* to do, I had to do.
I mean you, Peter, rock in my path.
My re-birth in rock, my two roots forced,
one diamond-bit down through the shelly layer.

I was my own vital stepping stone, under the aegis.
Everybody fought to fit through the astral gates.
My hair tangled in the blades and wrapped handles,
boot straps and sandal straps, hooves and ankles.

Get behind me. Jump

A Letter from Venerable Annapolis
Sister. I got up to go look at the beautiful woman.
She wore a striped and swimming shirt.
A sea wind ripped back every cover.
Cold cars of light rolled out on the island.
Light chose one wave and not another—

Mithras, *sol invictus*, invincible sun,
are you the protector of this empire? Or what?
I ask you from this city built on a swamp.
In the green arcades, the old deities are dying and rising
in their tennis whites, serving and falling.

I sent the elderly children out to throw onto the sea
the blossomy laughter of the pundits.
I have invented fustian again from scratch.

Let me be unto this world as the spinning jenny
as the pre-fab rifle.

Down at the Inner Harbor,
Myself, disguised, descending
the big white sightseeing boats and shiny water.

Space must be filled with food and flower vendors,
musicians, hammers, banners, fountains, fountainings
benches and plants must overflow the midblock plazas

I didn't pray, afraid, in all the carpenters and scaffolds
The Eucharist going on
The bells exploding with it

What is this color vision *for?*

King: To understand and love at the same time the victors
        and the vanquished like in *The Iliad*—
            God:—I guess I just want to be seen.

        I like the attention towards me. I like the activity. I like the noise.
        I like the people. I like the people who work there. I like the scenery.
        I like the schedule. I like the operations. They said I wasn't there.
        But I was there.

of course, all fires look the same up close.
the prisoners went free,
doves from a dovecote,

the heretics went scrambling through the tri-state,
the picked-over degrees of divinity
stashed in their packs. Brainchild,

they are still at large.
night has fallen. the stone lion
has flown up to the pillar over the square.

under the bull moon,
the train is leaving which will carry us into our fosterage.
daddy, pull me down from the train through the window.
griffin-sister, leap from my back.

Revelations/Celebrity Cribs

We're kicking out everyone who can't dance.
At the cops' third knock, we tour the mansion
on the arm of the drumming star. . .
Already the ground in the morning
is covered with 'what's-it-called'.
                    Manna, that means. Make a line
from Paul to the spectator, please.
It flows to the river and the animals eat it.

Which makes it—what?
If the judge merely *feels* the facts
and doesn't see with the eyes of his mind
the red Ferrari flooding the tubs of hotel palms,
Old Fear-and-Amazement falling from his horse,
the bell-boys engaged in lifting him
or fleeing in beautiful attitudes, a fleeing horse
dragging along One Who Seeks to Restrain It;
what had seemed a circular drive
abruptly ending—

The Mayor's Soliloquy

1.
What's made of paper cannot stand
a damp climate. The wet, fibrous
stroke of each hand's book of matches. I sent
my surrogate out in a train
wrapped with bunting. The colors
running. This was before
our tree became the national tree.

2.
It was cut down, no roots in a burlap ball
to travel along to the Capitol. The stump
remained, the tree became
unimaginable. The avenues lined
with double-eared parking meters.
The baby battened down
and strapped to a saucer was last year's
snow-experiment. That doesn't
count now. I'm watching the silver drift
on Sideboard Lake. It doesn't drift.

3.
We tried to take a plebiscite of Vermilion
County. We were met with a carillon
of whistles and coughs. A wind carried off
the card that told my weight. A frog in my throat
expressed disdain. All sleeves,
I want to change. Inform my surrogate.
You can see my head through my hair
in this light. You can tell by looking

Book Of

Then it was I drove into a low wall
gently, and my safetybelt held me
there in place.

Parking ramp. And the stitched vinyl
of the steering wheel gripped me
back. And the narrow band
of sky between that level and the next.

Isolated thunderstorms.
Grass fires double back for the river.

Chopper like a maple seed borne back up.
The subtle-hued skirt of ash and the hem of flame.

Newsflash. From Grand Central Terminal,
the candidate gestures his acceptance.

Breakthrough. A honeybee knows
its own destiny.
Cannot be fooled.

the setting sun fits in a tree
for this is Africa, where
a zebra colt folds

into a river.
Raises up its tufted head
one last time. Nothing
like fear in its eyes.

Endless veldt, maybe;
giraffes pitch themselves
towards the water.
Landlocked, lock-kneed,
their coats of islands.

A Proverb

A mammoth tantalus.
A burgeoning aftermath.
An evening performance at the Cancer Center.

In dialogue with the resonant fabric,
lettuce, I embrace you, and I admit
that internal suffering is difficult to photograph.
Lost toads, I call for you
in the back yard, I toe over the leaves.
little cha-cha

     It is a convention

of rogue biography to divorce and divorce
and to never get separate,
to give your children titles for first names, to lose
history, mid the brambles, the defile, we didn't have
to travel but kept meeting ourselves on the field
in vinyl, or in armor, or

one house-move equal to three fires.

The Voyage of the Beagle

Fisherman's Terminal!
The body recovered and the body re-
covered
and recovered. Seward's folly, this purchased
inner passage.

92 foot long arctic rose, rose of all the world,
but princ'p'ly Seward's, ourselves', which catches fish
on a series of hooks attached to long lines. . .

"I intend to come back to India for the rest of my life"—
(he's a big personality in the world)

Up on the seawall, the milkbottle ringing
the empty body sounding in the surf.
That is Atlantic, and not the unimaginable
("SICK")   ("NO LONGER")

I intend to come back for the rest of my life

The Voyage of the Beagle

If 55 countries representing 55 percent of
ratify the protocol,

then it begins to function.

kid, you don't seem very bright.
The faculty—
                    pan arcadia!—
the entire structure of Machu Piccu—
whole-lake re-imaging—
An accidental meeting in a delicatess

Outraged by rumours of corruption in his regime,
he tried to trace the root of everyone one.

le Absolue selon
le bourgeoisie absolue

Grow, little trees.
under the chalet's eaves.
which is the star of the subdevelopment.

                    —cars going by like dead air

The Voyage of the Beagle

Enters:
Disabled list.
          suspended. Home-confinement
outside
          handed a suspension.

for sixty days
          fivehundredthousand dollars
six months
          eighteen months

three hundred fifty thousand
twenty
          a year's
21
          a thirty
          two years'

The Voyage of the Beagle

A featherblade,
a leaf leached down to its vasculature

(coluratura)
by the weather or
(mallets) by
(tympanum) a

zillion dull blades mostly
missing the mark.

                  dovetails, tenons.
The governor will decide tomorrow what time it is
and then the planes will leave.

Lemice-Térieux   le mystérieux
that was his nom-de-plume.
still is, wherever plumes are worn.

watching cable.
this is the sac for my organs and eggs
I splice from regurgitated leaves,
St. Loop. Add a line, -by-line.
It's a ban, a non-response.

The Voyage of the Beagle

Most Ren. drawings are a bit later, but this one, executed in 1480,
is a bit earlier.

with some 400 obj. created by 156 ethnic groups,
it proceeds in clusters of related

nègre—ghostwriter
the term is in use today.
division of cycling enthusiasts
into two camps: *pro* and *contra*

Faculty of   (medicine)
author of   (a series of antisemitic works)

sink-apace.
      the Russian battle
for autonomous television

I am sure to be useful,
having always been

The Voyage of the Beagle

Mayor's Cup Youth Succour Fest Venetian Night Air and Water Show
outbound FRUIT KEY and twig key TRANSFER

model of the moment:
give me a new image of myself. an operation,
an opera commissioned by the Portuguese government
in celebration of the discoveries of its explorers (14th to 16th cee)

anaphylaxis network,
a "die-once-and-get-resurrected" plan for the economy. . .

It also calls upon companies
to list allergens by their "common
English" names. When they do appear on labels,
they are referred to by formal names: like
casein (milk) or albumen (eggs).

These names are greek. these labels,
written for scientists, not consumers.
DuPont has lots of wonderful brands, but it's struggling
with its long term business-vision.

DuPont, whose formal name is E. I. duPont de Nemours and Company
has made a decision

to walk away from the life science industry

The Voyage of the Beagle

It's an empty vessel but it may create an opening
        —Unlimited Homestead Exemption, Act for Swans
The women win in overtime thriller
        —the mute swan in england, nineteenfiftyone.

Now schoolgirls hurling stones.
Everyone angry!
New treasures for a New Site
inscrutable disciplines. . .

each of the neighbors looks at the others
and finds them wanting
        —and I indicated.
it breaks into human affairs like a moonprince.
once a man is through, his art is through, also.
prismatic elephant
-and-baby, 100 questions regarding dolphins, seasnails,
sponges, starfish, fishes, shorebirds, and others, women
walking, running, climbing, bending, turning,
et cetera,

The Voyage of the Beagle

eek eek I admit
ex-strongman, who the loss is: icummen
maestro, exchequer.

the longer it goes not finding him,
the scarier it gets.

last couple of days, everybody
been asking around
                    you got any update? you heard
                    anything? I just think, like, maybe,
                    you all have.

abused the numerous opportunities he had for freedom.

cellular cluster.
Radio'd the plane that had no pilot.
was in constant communication with the plane.
needed to get the *tree* into the *cab*
the tree in a net for delivery
the plastic twisted sharper til it shone—

The Voyage of the Beagle

Works by triangulation,
calculating the position of an object
based on its distance from several others.

Narrows the location down to two,
one of which rejected as nonsensical.

Out in space, for example.

We were brothers, we performed as
The Nicholas Brothers, our legs
in stove-pipe trousers, my brother
a drainpipe   nonagenarian
legs   in his lead-lined

In the first phase the mystery of the Person
comes into sight as a mere object in the world
of Things but transcending Things

—heavy as a texas steer hide. or light
as the soubrette. her sobriquet

Stereo

split The Sun Sessions into high and low.
Sun made the coast impossible
to see, a static flash, the visual field
impassable. The road wound on continuously
as if that were possible. Until we were
needlepointing up.

Up! Construction of this world
is a job for laymen: linens,
ramekins—a cake for each guest,
a souvenir mussel shell no one can touch,
a whorl working inward. A song to sing in bed.

My lights and my heavies, pray, take note:
the bees as clean as young French Christians
lifting from the thicket
as they may and might. They retain
the mark of excision, they are ready to receive
restitution. Caught in the pincerlike
motion of

this world—the beauty
pageant in the walled city,
the doctors without borders
taking this opportunity
to reorganize—the Sea Similized
to Pastures, the Mariners to Shepherds,
the Mast a Maypole, the Fish
Beasts—

Joy

1. sees everything in its place, including herself.

At the equally secretive
Institute for the Brain: Joy; a bomb-plot
at the Radisson hotel; a file of phone-bills
from the local cell.

The Jordanian plot is the *template*.
The Jordanian account is *accurate*, or so
officials have been persuaded.

Joy the Mortarman. Joy the American.

2. known only by her nom-de-guerre(s).

A fuse; a bulb in the mail. Above the double-hulled
basement shell, Joy buries the bulb in stones.
water blubs down. A leaky cask.
A flammable lake o'er the concrete bed
spreads. We walk above it.
Somehow, it doesn't ignite.

3. Joy; blub; The dreaming arranged
and the forged Gold Dealer's License
to avoid detraction, and the four separate routes to avoid;
and the bellwether perched on the little rise; one
of two hooves; ruminant; a grassy fall

4. *Rehearsal*:
Placards banging our chests.
Mine says *The Precedent*.

There was a house held up by plumbing.
There was a chimney house.
As we threw over it in the heliocopt.
As it happens, there were various skeletons
(of houses) and a dozen ties
and shirts in the back of the Chevrolet.
And there would be a deliverable inaugural
in exactly that many days.

5. the consciousness of a break, actual or impending.

Seated before the cerulean tank.
If there are criminals at all here, they're in the balconies.
And one in the front row waiting for a sign

6. actual and impending

Sleep Passages
In a finished world, sleep could not be waking.
could not be *distinguished from*
waking at noon. *nein* nine.
Non-consuming.

7. wake up to the auction of a doublebird jar.
sleep through the auction at the armory.
The beautiful antique lances
tilting into new lucky hands.

8. A three-part command to stand.
And if not, a command to stand.
And if not, a lifting.

9. A victrolling of my single, novelty hit. . .

10. And meanwhile, seated before the grid,
at least we gave the country what it wanted.
Lush crepe-covered blackouts
roll down the coast. Still, seated before the dolphin show,
separated from our *conditions of origin*
from a sense of *immediate living*
from the *genius loci*

or whatever

And then the grid explodes

11. And meanwhile, old chrysanthemum-head,
health-happy!
And meanwhile, old cormorant keeper,

Joy

Afterlives

*

Forsythia opens its bright palm
and the woman pushes her stroller out of it.

*

This festive littleness of food.
                              These spirits,
the color of glass, disappear
                              into what they're poured into.
This festive littleness of air.

*

But to walk out onto August's
                              speedy, undulating greens.

To be fast in the green of that fairway.

FENCEbooks

Zirconia
Chelsey Minnis
WINNER OF THE 2001 ALBERTA PRIZE

Miss America
Catherine Wagner

The Red Bird
Joyelle McSweeney
WINNER OF THE 2002 FENCE MODERN POETS SERIES

Can You Relax in My House
Michael Earl Craig

FENCE was launched in the spring of 1998. A biannual journal of poetry, fiction, art and criticism, *Fence* has a mission to publish challenging writing and art distinguished by idiosyncrasy and intelligence rather than by allegiance with camps, schools, or cliques. *Fence* has published works by some of the most esteemed contemporary writers as well as excellent work by the completely unknown. It is part of our mission to support young writers who might otherwise have difficulty being recognized because their work doesn't appeal to either the mainstream or to accepted modes of experimentation.

FENCEbooks is an extension of that mission; with our books we hope to provide expanded exposure to poets and writers whose work is excellent, challenging, and truly original. **The Alberta Prize** is an annual series administered by *Fence Books* in conjunction with the Alberta duPont Bonsal Foundation. The Alberta Prize offers publication of a first or second book of poems by a woman, as well as a $5,000 cash prize.

Our second prize series is the **Fence Modern Poets Series**, published in cooperation with **saturnalia books**. This contest is open to poets of either gender and at any stage in their career, be it a first book or fifth, and offers a $1,000 cash prize in addition to book publication.

For more information about either prize, visit our website at www.fencebooks.com, or send an SASE to *Fence Books*/[Name of Prize], 14 Fifth Avenue, #1A, New York, NY 10011.

To see more about *Fence,* visit www.fencemag.com